Handmade Forests

the treeplanter's experience

Hélène Cyr

NEW SOCIETY PUBLISHERS

Cataloguing in Publication Data

A record for this publication is available from the National Library of Canada and the Library of Congress.

All photographs ©1998 by Hélène Cyr, unless otherwise stated.
Photographs on pages 56, 66, 67, and 90 ©1998 by Martin Labelle.
Copyright of individual essays rests with the individual authors.
All rights reserved.

Cover design by Miriam MacPhail from a photograph by Hélène Cyr.

Printed in Canada on acid-free, recycled paper by Friesens.

ISBN 0-86571-393-6

To order directly from the publisher, please add $4.00 to the price of the first copy,
and $1.00 for each additional copy (plus GST in Canada). Send cheque or money order to:
New Society Publishers
P.O. Box 189, Gabriola Island, BC, V0R 1X0, Canada
Tel: 1-800-567-6772

New Society Publishers aims to publish books for fundamental social change through
nonviolent action. We focus especially on sustainable living, progressive leadership,
and educational and parenting resources. Our full list of books can be browsed on the
worldwide web at: http://www.newsociety.com

NEW SOCIETY PUBLISHERS
Gabriola Island, BC, Canada and Stony Creek, CT, USA

Contents

Acknowledgments

*This book is dedicated to Félix, Judith, and all the people
who have ever planted a tree or think of doing so.*

Heartfelt thanks to: John Cathro for his non-stop energy and brilliant spirit; Sioux Browning for her splendid talent and for being there since the beginning; Doug Plant for planting my trees in unforgiving land while I took pictures; Agence Stock Photo for introducing me to some amazing photographers; Vox Populi for their professional ways and dedication to photography; Félix Breault-Cyr for being so happy and patient; Jean-François Cyr for his humor and support through rough times; Judith Warrington for her courage and outstanding beauty; Rob Ursel for the funniest THOR joke ever and his influence on me to plant faster; Robert Chayer and Mance Lanctot, my best friends ever; Jean-Pierre Breault for lifelong memories; Dirk Brinkman for kindly accepting to write the foreword; Heather Wardle for her sensitivity and remarkable eye; Chris and Judith Plant for their view of life and generosity; John Betts for his efforts in the industry; David Boehm for sharing his funny stories; John McClarnon; Dave Wallinger; Rick Caulfield; Tom Severson; Alan Rycroft; David Stewart; Marie-Pierre Germain; Karen Pattington; Marielle Beaupré; Michael Mloszewski; Lori Marek; Sean Wilson; Marlene Dayman; Chris Sihoe; Martin Begin; Mountain Top Reforestation Ltd.; Denis Fraser Reforestation; and Natural Borders & Coastal Silviculture. Special thanks to photographer Martin Labelle for his photos on pages 56, 66, 67, and 90 and for the journey we took together with this project. Sincere thanks also to all the people whose names are not mentioned here.

The Regeneration Generation

A Foreword by Dirk Brinkman

One hundred years ago there were six billion hectares of forest worldwide. Today the remaining three billion are only shrinking in the tropics, though still at an alarming rate of 17 million hectares per year. Hélène Cyr's *Handmade Forests* celebrates the generation of front-line planters who turned the tide of deforestation in the northern hemisphere. *Handmade Forests* captures the spirit of treeplanter culture during the mid-'80s, the midpoint of the first regeneration generation.

For centuries, civilizations have risen and fallen based on a pattern of building on their forest resources and then sputtering out on their deforested deserts. As the latest region to emerge from the vital pioneer phase of historical development, North America now plants nearly two and a half billion trees per year. British Columbia has led the way in the practical implementation of ecosystem principles which guide treeplanting. Today in BC, professional treeplanters select the right species of tree for each spot based on microsite indicators, and sites are reforested with an ecologically suitable mix of tree species planted in natural patterns.

Hélène Cyr has documented the sort of planting crews that made that uniquely sustainable phenomenon possible. It was a period of high diversity in the treeplanting world when most of the photographs in this book were taken. Piece-rate pay systems, which began as a logical way to split the net revenue of the contract according to how many trees each person planted, evolved in BC's wilderness Galapagos of free enterprise, emerging through every experimental blend of cooperative and capitalist structure. Only the fittest, fastest, most flexible, and innovative individuals and systems survived.

In 1987, BC passed a silviculture regulation which required logging companies to reforest every area cut at their own cost, using ecologically appropriate species which had to be grown until they were free of competition. I lobbied hard for this regulation and it has gradually transformed treeplanting. Now crews are not just survivors of the "lowest-bid-wins" curse. They are valued for their quality of work, and many forester-contractor-treeplanter relationships have stabilized. During the last decade, more and more career treeplanters have made silviculture their place to stand in life.

Handmade Forests is being published at a crucial time. The harvest is shrinking in BC and the IWA (Industrial Wood and Allied Workers) now wants these forest jobs. In 1997 the BC premier planted the four billionth tree. But he was not celebrating veteran treeplanters. In fact, the BC government has joined the union in demonizing these unique professionals who follow the snowmelt from coast to interior, labeling treeplanters "itinerants, transients, and nomads." Now on the coast over half of the new silviculture work is required to go to laid-off loggers, who neither fit silviculture nor cultivate the fitness required.

Handmade Forests celebrates silviculture, a vibrant sub-culture as unique as logging and pioneering. It celebrates the people who survived and thrived in vertical slash, horizontal rain, blinding sweat, deafening mosquitoes, and maddening no-see-ums. This is the regeneration generation who took reforestation from a 60 percent seedling survival rate in monoculture plantations, to be on track for a 97 percent success rate in establishing ecosystem-appropriate plantations with species mixed by artists into natural eco-scapes. These trees don't just survive, they grow.

This is the first book, I hope, of a series, because there are many stories to tell.

Dirk Brinkman is the president of Brinkman & Associates Reforestation Ltd., the oldest and largest reforestation company in Canada, and the editor of the Canadian Silviculture Magazine.

Filling in the Empty Spaces

A Preface by Sioux Browning

In the vast open plains of the western United States there is a place where the license plates read "Big Sky Country." And it's true, the sky does roll out broadly over the sweet-grass prairie. But a question remains — is the sky bigger in a place where the land is naturally open like the grasslands, or does it seem bigger in a place where the land is exposed when it shouldn't be, naked in the brazen landscapes of a logged forest? This is a question which daily faces the thousands of treeplanters who pour into the British Columbia Interior every summer or the thousands of others who plant in northern Alberta and Ontario. Beneath their caulk boots is the debris of clearcuts. Before them are two views: the savaged remains of forest and the sky.

This book is about treeplanters and the way they occupy the forest's empty spaces. The photographer, Hélène Cyr, spent five years planting trees in northern and central BC and most of these images were taken during that time. But the quality of the experience is the same for treeplanters across Canada and the United States; it is monotonous, hard, painstaking work done in challenging weather on difficult terrain. It's horrible and yet most planters can't get enough of the job, returning year after year to reap treeplanting's varied rewards. Planting is much more than a seasonal job; it is a commitment to the bizarre world of putting trees back where they belong, where they had always been before, so they can eventually be taken out again. You understand you are not putting in a forest — you are putting in a crop and your body is the harrow, seeder, and manure spreader all in one. You try not to think of whether the crop will survive or fail, because it is beyond your control and you will get paid regardless. You will stand out there under that great big sky and you may realize that you love your job in a way you have never loved anything before. With every tree, you have planted a part of yourself.

Although the forest industry has experimented with reforestation since the 1930s, there is still a gold-rush mentality to the job. Camp life tends to the lawless. There is no curfew, no radar traps on the roads, no long arm of the law reaching out to curtail the consumption of booze or other substances. You live within the boundaries of communal tolerance, which can be high or low, depending on how the contract is going. Music tends to be alternative and varied. Personal hygiene levels fluctuate wildly, depending on the person, on the availability of a town with a laundromat, and on whether the portable showers are working.

You can make a lot of money planting trees, if you're good enough. The best of the best, the camp highballers, can hit the $300-per-day mark on a regular basis. Most planters average less than that, but it's still not a wage to sneeze at. It is piece work, so how much money you make depends on how much you plant. Speed is only a part of it; you are also paid by how well you plant each tree. If industry checkers find a fault in the samples or "plots" they throw in your area, you may get paid, say, 98 percent of the full price of the tree. If your quality falls below 85 percent, you have to go back over what you've done and replant it. Sloppiness costs money and time. Some companies pay every planter based on the crew's overall quality, so there is a lot of pressure to plant well. Payment also depends on the contract. If a clearcut is bid at ten cents per tree in reasonable soil and conditions haven't changed by the time the actual planters get to it, a lot of money can be made with relative ease. But if the bid is based on dry ground in the August heat and the planters are actually putting trees there in a rain-soaked, mosquito-infested bog nine months later, every dollar made feels like it takes a day off their lives. As hard as conditions can get, the money is still good enough to bring them back the next season or the next year.

Every camp contains an eclectic collection of people: students making fast money for their fall semester, ex-hippies still happy to be living on society's fringe, economic outcasts, young Easterners out west looking for adventure, new immigrants who have no other options until they command the language or qualify in their field, lifers who put in the time to take out the cash. Life as a treeplanter can be a trial. Virtually every minute of your day passes outdoors. A tent or van or the plastic walls of the cookshack may relieve you of the elements for a while, but they can't turn back the heat. In the rain or snow (in July), it's a fight to see who can sit in the crummy during lunch or who gets the closest to the lone camp stove.

Planters tend to live invisible lives, vanishing into the bush every spring and emerging months later with funny tan lines and bruised shins. It is life lived slightly outside the norm. Social graces that wear off in camp can be difficult to recover back in town. Some planters don't even try — they can wreak havoc on a place during a motel contract or while in town on their days off.

Personally, I never thought a tough job was an excuse to indulge in poor behavior; however I don't completely mourn the erosion of the patina of civilization that happens when you plant trees for a living. Something about the job and the lifestyle breaks you apart as a person and puts you back together again. If you survive the process and keep planting, you understand yourself better. You won't lie to yourself about anything. You learn what your body will and won't do, and you respect those limits. You learn what behavior you will accept from yourself and others. You simply face up to the difficult, because bitching won't change it, and it won't go away.

For enduring, you are rewarded. Peaceful bear encounters, great food, skinny-dipping in a remote lake on an afternoon off. Apricots. Sweet, clean laundry. A series of mind-blowing end-of-contract parties. Hackeysack on the helipad. The smell of wet spring earth as your shovel cracks it open. Northern lights. You are a member of a club made up of thousands and, when you meet, you understand each other's experience without having to discuss it. Planter's claw is your secret handshake.

This book is about the members of the club. Every photograph contains a fragment of the experience that is treeplanting. It shows us at work, at play, and at rest in the places where the trees used to be. If we do our jobs properly, there will be huge trees there again someday. The book is not intended as a commentary on the moral pros and cons of clearcutting. It isn't about the politics of the forest industry or an environmental gnashing of teeth. It is about people doing a job most other people don't think about. In a sense, it brings the treeplanting way of life out of the woodwork.

I think these photographs accurately depict the moods and imbalances of that life. The photographs are honest. They are fair. They do what they have to do. Mostly they show us out there, planting trees under that great big sky, bending toward the earth, filling in the empty spaces.

Sioux Browning is a writer and recovering treeplanter. She has a Masters degree in creative writing from the University of British Columbia and is a former editor of the award-winning literary quarterly PRISM *international. Her poetry has appeared in the anthology* Breathing Fire: Canada's New Poets.

A Hundred Years on the Block

by Sioux Browning and Dave Wallinger

"Down there in Hades, Sisyphus thinks about the treeplanters and thanks his lucky stars every day because he has such a soft gig." — Robert Heilman, from his essay *Overstory: Zero*

Treeplanting takes place within an ever-expanding series of concentric rings. It begins with the seed, harvested from a cone, then leads to the test tube where the seedling is grown, to the "microsite" or patch of exposed dirt where the seedling is planted, to the plot of land the planter is given to fill, to the "block" or clearcut which contains the plot, to the forest district containing the clearcut, to the province or state which governs the forest district, and finally, to the biggest ring of all, the global timber market.

The job of treeplanting would not exist without logging. Since Europeans first stepped on North American soil, trees have been cut down and floated off the continent to foreign destinations. The massive oaks of Ontario and the eastern seaboard of the US became European warships and freighters and sturdy furniture. From the late 1700s to the mid-1800s, the giant Douglas firs of the Pacific Northwest were also logged to provide spars for shipbuilding. The invention of the steam locomotive and the explosion of rail travel in the 19th century created a huge demand for railway ties across the continent.

But it was the series of gold rushes in the west, starting in California in 1847, that truly fired the engines of the timber industry of BC and the Pacific Northwest. Cities sprang up almost overnight, changing from tent villages hacked out of the bush to rough urban centers with saloons, churches, boardwalks, and thousands of people keeping the demand for wood at a fever pitch. The need for building materials and firewood was filled by loggers using only single-bit axes and oxen-powered skidder teams.

The American Civil War put a crimp in things for American loggers, disrupting US exports to Europe and Asia. Meanwhile, the demand for lumber from the Prairies, California and markets further afield — China, South America, Hawaii, and Australia — continued to grow. The end of the Civil War meant temporary prosperity for the forest industry on both sides of the border. By the 1890s, the Pacific Northwest went into a recession and the BC mills took the opportunity to ship even more timber to the California market. The second wave of gold rushes in Alaska and the Klondike eased the pinch and things progressed until the

First World War, when all exports ceased due to German presence in the Pacific. But soon the war effort began to generate its own demand for wood products.

As early as the turn of this century, there was concern in the US over dwindling hardwood timber supplies. This concern generated interest in California in planting eucalyptus trees: the species' quick growth and ability to sprout from cut stumps were seen as ways to meet increased demand for wood. Over 60,000 acres of eucalyptus were planted in California in the early part of the century, but when the wood was actually harvested, it did not perform to its expected potential. Attention again turned to the Pacific Northwest and BC to provide much-needed timber.

With the huge numbers of trees being taken out of the lush forests of the Pacific coast and inland, eventually the need arose to reforest logged areas. While histories of the "good ol' days" of logging crowd the bookstore shelves, little information exists on the early days of treeplanting. This is partially because treeplanting is a relatively new phenomenon, younger than bottled colas and older than computers. It takes a while for industry insiders to become reflective and commit their memories to paper. Partially it is because, unlike logging, the approach to treeplanting differs across the continent.

Trees were planted on an experimental basis across Canada as early as the 1920s and slightly earlier in the US. Changes in forest technologies in the 1950s initiated larger-scale production of seedlings. By the 1970s, it became clear that years of traditional logging practices were resulting in environmental damage (erosion, destruction of watersheds, loss of wildlife habitat etc.) which prompted provincial, state, and federal governments to change policies and increase the regulations governing forestry. Treeplanting became a critical component of new forestry practices. Currently, forest companies can sign agreements with provincial or state governments to log, replant, and manage sections of land on their own while still complying with government regulations. Other companies can log federally owned lands and pay a stumpage fee to the government, which then uses the money for

reforestation. Planting jobs are contracted out to treeplanting companies through a variety of bid systems.

This is a book about treeplanting in industrially logged areas of BC primarily, but treeplanting has deeper roots and wider scope. For instance, in the US treeplanting is often more of an urban concern. There are an estimated 69 million acres of urban forests in the US and treeplanting is widely regarded as a civic duty. Arbor Day, which began in 1870 in New England and increased in popularity until it was declared a national holiday, encourages the tradition of urban treeplanting. Beyond that, croplands that are considered highly subject to erosion or are otherwise environmentally sensitive may be voluntarily retired (as part of a US Farm Bill Conservation Reserve Policy) and planted with trees and shrubs. In California, where a considerable percentage of the natural flora is made up of introduced species, parks and public lands managers have begun treeplanting programs to help restore indigenous landscapes.

A significant example of early reforestation took place on Angel Island in the San Francisco

Bay area. For 83 years (1863 to 1946), the island served as a military base, detention camp, and an immigration and quarantine station. In 1942, a planting project was started to counteract erosion. Anthony Julis was hired to oversee the project: "We secured seedlings from the Federal Soil Conservation Service. John Harriston, the foreman, got a shovel gang and took [the trees] into the hills and planted them: 45,000 trees in three years. There were cork oaks from the Iberian Peninsula of Spain, black locust, Monterey pine, ponderosa pine, redwood, Douglas fir, and many kinds of shrubs ... We planted the big trees to go down deep and the small stuff to hold the surface soil immediately."

Whatever the incentive for planting trees, the process remains the same. Dig a hole, take care handling the roots, close the hole properly, and then nature does the rest. The practice of treeplanting hasn't always been regarded as natural though, particularly in the eyes of early forest company managers and others whose interests were at stake. There were many instances where the act of planting trees was met with resistance. For instance, in 1957 the Burns Logging Company held a Tree Farm License in BC's Slocan River valley. The professional forester overseeing the license, John Murray, asked the nearest Forest Service Nursery to supply him with seedlings; 14,000 Douglas fir seedlings were shipped to him and planted. When the company owner discovered a planting crew working on his license, he was less than enthralled with this "new-fangled" idea. When he received the bill for the planters' wages, he nearly fired Murray for "wasting" company money.

Other parties were also not too keen to have planters fill in logged areas which were in use as cattle range. For instance, the planting of ponderosa pine on old cutblocks did not sit well with the cattle-ranching community in parts of BC. They saw the open range as theirs and they feared that, as the pines got larger, the needle drop would choke out the grass. They fought the planting program vigorously — even to the point of going out to the planted areas in the evening and pulling up the trees which had been planted that day.

While the history of logging and seedling production in North America is one of ever-advancing technology, the history of treeplanting is one of stripped-down, almost pre-industrial techniques. Treeplanting requires a planter, trees, a bag to carry the trees, and a tool to plant them with. Planting machines, while in existence, don't have a prominent place in contract-driven treeplanting. A machine planter, which was pulled behind a tractor, was used on an experimental basis in BC in 1953. Its double-footed ploughshare opened a furrow, the operator placed seedlings into the furrow, and the machine closed the trench. The operator could put in 7,500 to 10,000 trees per day this way. However, it was useless in rocky soils or on slopes greater than 15 percent. Given that most western cutblocks occur on rocky, steep terrain, it was inevitable that this machine would fall out of favor.

Transportation and methods of tree handling have all benefited from new technologies. Seedlings are now stored in refrigerated trucks or "reefers," and more areas are accessible to planters by helicopters, boats, and quads (four-wheeled all-terrain vehicles). Site preparation has made a difference in both planting efficiency and tree survival. Broadcast burns (where the cutblock is essentially napalmed in order to burn the slash), trenching, furrows, scarification (where the ground is machine-prepared in various sized trenches to reveal mineral soil), and windrows (where the slash is pushed aside to create giant alleys of accessible soil): these are a few of the ways that technology has made it easier for planters to do their jobs. As for the act of planting itself, the tools would not have looked out of place in the Middle Ages. Bags hang from the hips. Trees are stuffed in the bags. In BC and Alberta, most seedlings are "plugs," in which the tree roots are encased in a test-tube-shaped cylinder of organic matter. In Ontario and Oregon, bare-root seedlings are still in use, in which case the roots are kept moist and alive by dipping them in "slurry" which is either a special chemical preservative or mud from the nearest puddle.

In Canada, the planting tool of choice has changed over the years. Until the mid-1970s, trees were planted with a mattock. As forest scientists tinkered with seedlings, planters used dibbles, planting guns, and narrow shovels. Occasionally, they used US-style hoedads, which are still used in Washington and Oregon. The hoedad, or grubhoe, is a special blade mounted on an adze handle and is best suited for planting on steep terrain. The tool used almost exclusively by Canadian planters now is the shovel, with either a D-handle or a long staff. Most planters modify their shovels, shortening and cushioning the handle and narrowing the blade, until it suits them perfectly. Some planters even devise "spoons" for steep terrain — this is basically a blade and a handle with no wooden shaft. Planting bags have also evolved, from a single burlap sack with a strap to wear over one shoulder, to a heavy-duty, two- or three-sack, plastic-coated creation with adjustable, padded straps for the shoulders and hips. Special liners are inserted into the bags to keep seedlings moist, cool, and protected.

Early treeplanting crews were made up of men recruited off the streets. By the 1960s, nursery production had increased to the point that a more dependable labor force was required. In BC, the first planting contracts were awarded in 1970. The contractors brought a flood of university and college students in to work. Where the governments didn't contract out the work and ran their own crews instead, First Nations planting crews, former housewives, and inmate crews made up a percentage of the workforce.

In BC, Alberta, and Ontario, the job has become a kind of sub-culture. Planters tend to be categorized as a certain kind of person, much like hippies were in the 1960s and '70s. The early days of contract planting were particularly colorful. Crews operated under names like "Pure Land and Human Hand" or "Flatulent Silviculture." Some contractors changed the names of their companies every year. A number of the early contractors have thrived for years; many, led by less astute businessmen, were doomed to fail.

Treeplanting in Canada has become a rite-of-passage for many young people. The current planting population is diverse. There are crews made up of strictly new immigrants, crews of friends who have planted together for years, and all-female crews. With changes in the forest industry, such as the Forest Practices Code in BC, the face of planting may change again to include many former loggers. In the US, planting crews are much like logging crews: they drive to the site from the mill in the morning and back home to their families at night. Back in 1953 in BC, the planter's wage was 47 cents per hour for a 48-hour work week. Many US planters are still paid by the hour (albeit with a much better wage), but Canadian planters do piece work. They are paid for the number of trees they plant and for the quality of their planting. How much money they make depends on how a contract was bid, the quality checking, the terrain, the weather and on how well the show is organized. Surviving life as a treeplanter may provide bragging rights back in the "real world," but planters are like every other forestry worker out there in the bush getting rain in his lunch box. They are there to do a hard job and make good money doing it.

North American lumber and pulp and paper markets have been a part of a global economy since European sailors knocked over their first oak. For more than a hundred years, sales to the Pacific Rim have been crucial to the state of the industry. At present, a terrific case of Asian "economic flu" has put a serious damper on the forest industry, causing massive cutbacks and lay-offs. Trade and tariff agreements on lumber have been a scrapping point between Canada and the US since the 1840s, with the latest versions taking shape as an ongoing softwood lumber dispute and debates over the North American Free Trade Agreement. All these economic concerns affect treeplanters too: when annual allowable cuts are reduced for any reason, fewer trees are planted as a result.

Change is afoot within the planting community as well. In recent years there has been a movement to unionize treeplanters in BC, a change which would radically alter the face of the industry. It would mean greater consistency in health and safety standards in camp, standardized pay and better organization for the planters, and fewer fly-by-night planting companies. However, it would also mean the renegade nature of the job would vanish. Its larger-than-life mythological aspects would dwindle in the face of equalizing bureaucracy. Unionization may, ultimately, be a boon to the planting community as a whole, but many planters are loath to surrender those elements of their jobs which distinguish them from the working population in general. Only time will reveal how the issue is resolved.

It is impossible to know what the state of treeplanting will be a hundred years from now. Perhaps there will be planters out there on the cutblocks slotting trees into holes using space-age tools or perhaps the whole industry will have ground to a halt. Perhaps planters will be putting in trees solely for environmental reasons and not just for logging purposes. One thing is certain — reforestation will be increasingly critical for the health of the planet. Billions of trees have been planted in North America in the last century; they are a testament to the hard work and dedication of the treeplanters.

Sioux Browning's biographical note appears on page 10. Dave Wallinger is a pioneer of the reforestation industry and a former silviculture specialist with the BC Forest Service.

Field Guide to the Treeplanter's Experience

by John Cathro

screefing

Screefing is the first thing learned, the last word spoken about treeplanting. Without even uttering the word, treeplanters are talking about it, or rather how to reduce the amount required. Screefing is all about removing the organic layer above the soil, about gardening a microsite for the seedling. Screefing is at best one or two supple swipes dug down to dirt, just enough to satisfy the checker. Screefing is at least a kick with the foot called a bootscreef, or the funky chicken if applied across a wide area.

Screefing is the bones of the operation. In tough ground the ability to locate and prepare a plantable spot is what makes someone a highballer. In open dirt you can plant screef-free. In moderate ground there is just enough diversity to ensure that the brain must remain engaged. The mind expands into the zone, a blend of obscure lyrics, the faces of old lovers, the bodies of potential new ones, flash-backs from previous contracts, previous lives. Not so much a case of life passing before one's eyes as significant episodes played and replayed, from one tree to the next, the exertion squeezing the meaning through pounding veins to drip from the forehead onto the ground.

Screefing is definitely not required in a type of cutblock know as a creamshow: soft, open dirt without rocks or roots or slash, where trees practically plant themselves every two and a half meters. Sometimes creamshows appear for hundreds of hectares in every direction and pay less than a nickel per tree. Sometimes cream occurs along roadsides or on ridges in more expensive ground. Thirty-cent dirt shots. This is where karma kicks in.

Planting cream is too good for words. This is where voices are raised, boundaries are disputed. A highballer is someone who turns every piece into a creamshow. Some planters muddle through the softest silkiest cream like they were standing still. Being creamed out is the ultimate invasion. Being labeled a creamer is the only true insult.

What is most interesting about cream is not what it does to piece-work planters but rather what it indicates ecologically. A minimally modified forest can have an organic layer several inches or more than a foot deep, not to mention bushes and weeds and moss and natural regeneration. That's a lot of screefing. Open dirt, on the other hand, is generally not a sign of forest soil health, especially over large exposed areas. But that's where the "best" planting is.

If an area is logged, burned, and then bulldozed into beach-like submission, a good planter could pound in four or five hundred trees an hour. But the likelihood of erosion is high, especially on steep ground, and without any organic layer or thermal protection the conditions can be extreme. Fast planting equals ecological disturbance. Creamshows are sometimes returned to year after year, each successive planter placing this year's offering in last year's screef.

breakfast

In spite of the all-encompassing complexities of the job itself, it is the camp that best defines treeplanting. More specifically, it is the kitchen. Oh, what the hell ... the entire effort rotates around the cook. The food is more important than the tree price, the weather, physical pain, or insurable weeks. The day begins and ends in the kitchen, and the cook is there to say good morning to you and to tuck you in at night.

Breakfast is served as early as 4:30. The cook has been up for an hour or two, and the music blends with the aroma as planters arrive wiping sleep from their eyes. Adults who tear through the slash with the greatest of ease stand at the lunch table like they were five, teddy bears in tow, jammies hanging down, making sandwiches or just standing in a daze.

Breakfast is usually a selection of fried veggies, the bacon-egg thing, potatoes, omelets, fried tofu, muffins, fruit salad. Hot and cold cereal. Cigarettes. Maybe a joint out in the dry tent. Toaster doing double time. The cook either staying on top of it all or else sinking fast. Foremen drawing up lists, gathering their thoughts, collecting their crews. A thermos filled with last night's soup. Another thermos filled with tea and honey. The cook trying to keep up with the incoming flow of rhythmically warming bodies.

Some are fed and gone before others arrive. The pace of the day establishing itself. Weather being weighed against the piece that lay ahead. A hackey-sack makes its rounds out by the trucks. Bong going round in the opposite direction. *Where's my shovel? Where's my dog? What truck was I in yesterday? Can you wait while I run to my tent and grab a cassette?*

Sun coming up. Dogs barking. Maybe this is on the shores of some pristine lake, or in the parking lot of a motel on the highway out of town. Breakfast is the same.

crummies

Crummies are trucks, driven to work, over bad roads, with names like Suburban, or Pig and Fist. Sometimes crummies take on the personalities of those who ride them, those who live there. Sometimes they are just trucks, rattling off to work full of planters. The stereo is more important than if it's new, or kicks butt, or needs to get pushed through the mud every now and then. Maybe it's a rental. Maybe it's a diesel. Maybe it's more like a car on the inside.

Crummies are like home base in kick-the-can, a refuge in the heat of battle, a place to beat the rain at the end of the earth, a hotbox, a home for all who care to move in. Sunk back in Stanfield comfort, boots off, heater blaring, the conversation changes with each bump in the road. Deep and heartfelt, sharp and critical, light and ironic. On a spur road or on the highway, a truck full of voices going on about slash piles and bear stories and old lovers.

There is a number out there that compares the amount of paved road built and maintained by the Department of Highways to logging roads pounded out into the bush by the Ministry of Forests. It's unbelievably disproportionate. All these logging roads branching off from paved highways, snaking up into valleys, crossing rivers on wooden bridges. Roads into cutblocks no one can drive to, a boat ride away, to crummies waiting on the other side.

Logging roads have taken their toll on crummies through flats and rocks and getting stuck. And sometimes worse than this. Maybe the crummy's CB radio doesn't work and it's either the ditch or straight at the logging truck coming around the corner. Or maybe you have to walk thousands of miles back to the highway because someone forgot the tire iron.

Or coming back to camp from town late at night after a playoff game and finding out the hard way that the bridge is gone. There was a time when treeplanting had the highest per capita fatality rate in the country because of all the road kill. Bouncing along with a bong in the back. Stereo blaring. Kablooey.

bagging up (part one)

There is an indescribable feeling pulling up on to a landing at the end of some logging road knowing that the long warm ride is over and the work is about to begin. The trip to the block is always different, always the same. Not such a great stereo drowned out by the heater or the wipers in the rain, by open windows in the summer. Bouncing along a dirt road digesting breakfast and the day ahead.

Six harmonious moans roll out when the crewcab jolts to a stop. The rain pounds on the roof of the rig, washing down the windows, and you're inside wishing that you didn't have to go outside. Socks already wet and the fog is blowing past. A feeling that you'd give what you made yesterday to simply roll over and go back to sleep. The thought of bagging up even once is frightening. Four runs is unimaginable.

Somebody opens the door and lets out a scream as a fist of wind smashes into the truck. Another door is opened and the crossbreeze makes rolling a smoke impossible. The point is to slip deeper into the back seat. You get a fleeting mental glimpse of other people everywhere doing normal things, being totally warm and dry, not about to break softly into tears.

Simply grabbing your gear from the back of the truck results in you getting completely soaked. Toes already doing that sploosh sploosh thing. Rain running cold down the neck, along the spine, through the crack of the ass. Wet wind so strong that it's hard to breathe.

It is widely understood that, at a certain temperature, and given the proper moisture levels, fingers simply disconnect from the brain. It happens unexpectedly and is sometimes accompanied by the sound of a guitar string breaking. Of course, feeling like this is better than the dizzying heat-stroke, dust, and bugs that can drive anyone insane, making a real cold sleet storm seem like a mirage. Strange thing is, you can get both of these extremes in the same day.

Sometimes it hurts more than it should. Struggling through the slash. Impossible to see where the last tree's planted. Fiddling with the roots. Getting caught on a stick. Finally jamming one in only to look over and see that it's less that a foot away from another. Yanking it out. Getting nowhere. Too hot or too cold. Too many bugs. Pain that travels like a moving creature from joint and muscle to its place just behind the eyes. Brutality.

the workplace

There are about a million hectares clearcut each year in Canada. There is no other word for it than clearcut. Not easy to put into words, though everyone seems to be talking about them. They carve a groove in the brain, day after day, as far as the eye can see. Oozing from the pores in the form of black and red slime. They are always the very worst-case scenarios. Three thousand hectares big. From ridge to shore. Twenty-foot-high piles of logs on the landing waiting to be burned.

It's amazing that more people aren't hurt. Slippery logs, sharp branches, loose rock in caulk boots. Most injuries are caused by givin'er shit. Tenosynovitis. Carpal Tunnel Syndrome. The claw. Pulled muscles and stiff necks and twisted joints. Sunburn. Hangover. Trikes, the now outlawed three-wheeled vehicles that were useful for transporting people and trees in the bush, used to claim twice as many victims as all other occupational accidents combined.

Intensive silviculture is required most where the natural limits have been exceeded. A fair number of clearcuts grow back naturally. Some areas are logged with great sensitivity and foresight. But you never work there. Instead it's a two-hour drive up the valley where the soil has washed off the rocks, the stumps are ten feet across, or the deer browse is so bad you'd have to build a fence to keep the lovely darlings away.

The strongest feeling you get is a sense of resilience. Moss growing from a crack in a rock. Naturals growing out of dead wood. Bushes and flowers and insects and mushrooms and animals. Big animals. The industry suggests that clearcuts mimic nature, that bears prefer the new openings in the forest. But nature acts like she doesn't really give a shit. Pour on the gas and let it burn so hot that the soil is baked hard. Next spring the green appears. It may not grow immediately into what we call economical timber, but we couldn't stop it from growing back if we tried. And we've tried.

human landscapes

The entire forest industry is dominated by men, as is almost all natural resource sector employment in Canada. Logging camps can be dozens of men and no women. Or maybe just the cook is female. Men living together for weeks on end, like soldiers who take time off from the front to visit their families.

Treeplanting is different. It is not uncommon to have as many men as women in a camp of 25. Rarely does a crummy leave with only men. The work is obviously physical but requires a separate form of toughness. Suppleness and mental focus are far more valuable than mere physical strength. More a question of coordination than cardiovascular capacity.

Women don't compete as rigorously as men. Women create a more nurturing atmosphere by working more cooperatively. For them, quality is not usually something to explore the minimal limits of, but rather an unquestioned part of the overall picture. Women, by their presence alone, make men behave themselves. Crude jokes just don't happen much. And oh, the love affairs.

Because treeplanting is not just a bunch of guys in a pick-up truck, it has become a lifestyle choice. It's not just a job, it's a family thing. As such, it attracts a wide range of individuals. Students, foreigners, doctors, musicians, travelers, dreamers, outcasts, weirdos, the insane, the pure. Camps often have daycare, a masseuse, electric guitars, video, a babbling brook, vegan dishes, lots of dogs, no smoking in the cookshack, great shitters, hot showers. Twelve people, maybe 70. One cook or two.

The one who plants twice as much as everyone else could easily go unnoticed in a police line-up. It's not the big jock or the peace-loving vegetarian necessarily. A lot of the top planters smoke a lot of pot. Finger-sized bombers on the landing between runs. Always at the end of the road. Rain coming down.

Or in the city, back on the farm. Hanging out together like a tribe. Shooting pool and telling bear stories, Berlin stories. To the point that everyone you know is a treeplanter. Or has been one. Maybe now a lawyer, a producer, a back-to-the-lander, but always just another ex-treeplanter. You'll recognize them in the laundromat. T-shirts worn and torn in all the right spots. To match the tan from last summer.

greeners

Anybody's first time planting is almost certainly the first time for a lot of other stuff as well — the first time in a clearcut, the first time washing your hands in the ditch before sitting down to inhale a sandwich, the first time doing bong hits at sunrise in the back of a crewcab, the first time watching mama bear and two cubs scamper back into the trees.

The rookies on the crew have a hard time blending in right away. Clothes too clean, hands too soft, posture just a little too eager and earnest. Losing the gee-whiz bewilderment is no easy task. Rarely does it immediately get scuffed and torn, or lost like lunch in the back of the truck. It drags on, painfully. Shiny and polite and very gentle. Awkwardly looking for a spot. Tentatively addressing the soil. Struggling with getting the roots in and the tree straight and the shovel out of the hole. Not doing such a great job of looking casual. Great care being taken to pat the cute young thing into place. A gentle tug to test the tightness and the earth breaks away. Stamp it again. Stop to wipe the brow. One more tug to be sure, and ... the top breaks off.

Only half of all greeners will be back the next year, and of those who return, most will not become career planters. The early dropouts can be found everywhere across the country — in a Yellowknife bank or a Queen Street café or beside you on a bus. It would be fair to say that everyone in Canada knows somebody who knows somebody who is a treeplanter. Or has been at one time.

The green phase is not measured in minutes or dollars. There are no courses to take or certificates to earn. There is no prescribed process to become, magically, a planter. Greeners become planters on that first cold morning with the sound of rain on the tent when the aching body absolutely refuses to get up and pull on wet clothes, but the mind and soul find themselves standing at the lunch table anyway, giggling.

shovels

As tools go, there are few equivalents in shape, appearance, or attachment. A tool so deeply loved and so badly beaten, polished smooth by constant bashing. A tool so cherished that you would never lend your best one to just anybody. A personal connection between the planter and planting device. Only *you* can smash it into rocks, roots, and roadsides.

Like an elongated limb, articulated at the hand, the shovel is a direct extension of the arm. With immaculate precision, and power enough to split a log, the shovel links the brain to the earth.

In a full-on groove through rocky ground, shovel control is the difference between getting trees in the dirt and simply standing around tapping on stones and growing miserable. On fast, open ground, the shovel becomes the ultimate hole maker, carving slim slits the perfect depth every time. In knee-deep boreal moss — sphagnum on the edge of a swamp

— no shovel is required. Just stick your hand into the cool wet depths and squeeze the puppy home.

After at least one good long contract, shovels are as unique as those who hold them. A demure long-handled staff with a long narrow blade for the tough ground with boulders and big slash. This would have the handle near the butt end worn thin from muddy hands slowly sanding the hardwood to a sheen.

Or a big mean D-handle with one of the kickers ground off to avoid getting snagged on roots and vines and branches. The blade is not only cut and shaped by hand to provide the most useful form, it is also getting retooled every time a tree goes in the ground until it shines.

The other possibility is a sawed-off little speed spade, with the tip so close to the handle that it's basically just a souped-up trowel. This particular shovel configuration facilitates some of the fastest planting known to humankind, the planter ever in a stoop, most of the action happening in the wrist and in the toe, going faster than the average person walks the dog. Four or five trees per minute all day long.

In any camp across the country you could line up all the shovels of the experienced planters and a blind person could match the tool to the individual based only on the tone of voice, the grooves on the shaft, the firmness of the handshake, and the balance of the blade to the handle as measured vertically on one finger.

shovel for hire

There are hundreds, if not thousands, of silviculture contractors across Canada. Most of them specialize in planting, with a little brushing or spacing on the side to fill out the season. Brushing involves beating back the bush after the trees have been planted so that ferns and fireweed do not squash the seedlings. Spacing involves going through an overstocked block with a powersaw and removing all but the healthiest trees. Some contractors consist of one truck, six planters, and a few thousand trees near town each spring. Others have offices in three provinces, dozens of big crews, secretaries, corporate structures, web pages, and enough pick-up trucks to open a dealership. Most people who stick with planting for a while work for both of these, as well as everything in between.

There has always been a certain mercenary quality about the typical treeplanter. Loyalty is not defined by the number of years of dedicated service, but by the quality of the planted tree and the relative ease with which the contractor can employ this individual. Very fast prima donnas almost have to be related to the boss to be kept around very long. Attitude is more important than attendance.

It's common to have a reputation as both someone to be counted on to return for the next season, and someone who works for three or four different contractors in the same year. Sporadic contract work demands flexibility, patience, and maybe even a set of wheels to get down the road or over to Alberta for the next contract.

From the perspective of a greener looking for that first job, contracts are always full. From the perspective of a planter, there is always room for a couple more people, especially if they plant good trees or play guitar and don't mind sleeping on the floor of the hotel room until a bed comes available.

Unless you have an in with someone, you start out working for whoever offers the first job, typically some generic northern volume-based penny contractor who recruits on campuses. An allegiance may develop if the planter makes it past the first week and if the contractor doesn't go broke, go insane, or disappear with all the money. Usually, the objective is to get out of the low-bid world of endless flat clearcuts and pine-spruce lunacy. Find somewhere with a bit of diversity — some mountains out west, or farm fields turned hardwood grove in southern Ontario. To become upwardly mobile is to have enough contracts linked up from spring to fall, or during the summer break.

After a few years of planting with a couple of different contractors, it begins to feel like everybody in the business is related, like you could just walk into any contract in the country and know someone there, or at the very least meet someone who knows someone you used to plant with. The fluid nature of planters moving between contracts means that when two planters meet on a beach in Thailand they will almost certainly, after only a couple of beers, trace their common lineages back to the very same cutblock.

bagging up (part two)

There's an indescribable feeling that you get planting trees when everything falls into place. Moving through uneven terrain, the shovel itself sniffing out the best plantable spot, spaced from all others, respecting young naturals deep in the slash for coverage. Seedlings practically planting themselves. Dirt shots appear between the arms of a stump. Each baby tree vacates the bag quickly as the hole opens with a stab push twist, burying to the root collar, back-cut, kick and onto the next. Like it takes longer to describe than to do.

Covering ground. Crawling through the mud and the limbs of what remains. The same old thing over and over. Focused on everything. Distracted by nothing. In this regard planters are Canada's version of the Saharan farmer or Thai rice planter. Precision movements again and again. Each task broken down to essentials. A familiarity with the earth that comes with cracked skin and frozen fingers.

Working hard. The heartbeat accelerating and then leveling off. The action from beginning to end continuous and fluid and performed with aesthetic minimalism and much elegance. Jamming the little buggers in everywhere. Contract spacing that can be performed while sleeping. Stocking standards established in some office somewhere, implemented with much grace among the squalor.

And then you bag out and stop and look up to see where you have just bagged out. The layered hill in the distance to infinity, green very clearly becoming blue, the wind chasing rain up the slopes. Calculating, on your way back to the cache to bag up and burn one, how much, at an hourly rate, this works out to be. Not believing the sum and checking the figures. Stepping over a log and forgetting all about it.

nine more days

In the block, something happens to time. It bends and expands and disappears. Time accelerates through good ground with hardly a moment to think, fluid from spot to spot. In shnarb the slash and stones snag and grab, pulling you back, hooked in the bags like fingers. Standing still against all odds, against the will, and even the wind refuses to budge.

Time is measured in several ways, depending on the circumstances: by the tree when the going is slow, and it seems like the bags will never be empty; by the bundle of ten or 20 when the going is good; by the run to calculate daily earnings; by the shift to find out how long the contract is going to last. Contracts are linked together to form a season. And then all the seasons blend together in the past to form a single event.

In the time it takes to make one very clean fast run of 240 trees, decisions can be made for the next ten years. The range of emotion and temperature and terrain between breakfast and dinner is dizzying. Shifts get stacked against one another to span several seasons. But it's all measured one tree at a time. Each tree exactly the same as the last, each tree completely different.

Contracts vary in size and duration, but generally contain just enough time to fall in love, get dumped, buy a truck, and fall in love again. For someone foolish enough to leave real life behind, a medium-sized contract up north can be pure, uncut hell. Just enough isolation to cause insanity, plus the ever-present possibility of maybe walking out to the highway and thumbing home. Wouldn't be the first time.

calories

Think of it as a license to eat anything. Burning up four or five thousand calories per day — similar to Olympic cross-country skiers, they say. And, if the groove is right, the constant attempt to go faster than the last run. Faster, always faster.

The appetite expands to fill the shape of the hunger. Four bowls of Shreddies before bed. A dozen cookies with a cup of tea beneath a tarp out of the snow on the landing. Five sandwiches per day is not unheard of. A joint at each bag up, run after run, year after year. An infinite quantity of beer, never soothing an unquenchable thirst. All of this more fuel for the next day on the block. The harder you work, the hungrier you get. The more you consume, the more you plant. With gallons of water to wash it all down.

Strange talents emerge. The ability to roll a

smoke mid-run in the pouring rain. An instinct to do absolutely everything else in life as efficiently as possible with no wasted moves. An advanced form of personal hygiene that cuts through the mud and the sweat and the bug juice.

Chemicals play a large, albeit mysterious, role in the whole equation. Applied by hose to huge greenhouses full of genetically altered baby trees, all of them cousins. And no one on the crew, including the company checker, knows what they're called or what they do. It says on every box of trees to wash your hands before eating, not to smoke while handling trees, to wear gloves. The point being that these little trees aren't exactly organic vegetables.

Typical tree handling is not like the box says. It's more like this: catch some air off the cutbank and toss the shovel one full rotation to stick in a log on the landing. Sproing. Huffing as the bags are dropped, a box is torn into, fistfuls of bundles. The whole time bent over double, head in the box, kneeling half inside of it, breathing heavily at the end of a run. Wash our hands? Where, in the ditch? Might as well spread the shit on your toast in the morning.

But there is always a certain sense of immortality, like it goes in one pore and out the other, as if to say: I can take this and more. This part of the job is contagious — it comes from the earth.

the federal minister of finance

In the crummy coming home, around the fire at night, in the city at the end of the contract, the conversation inevitably drifts back to the bid price, the tree price, the day rate, the dole, and finally back to Revenue Canada. A typical season is 15 weeks of work, perhaps $250 a day, rarely more than a hundred days a year. Stories of thousand-dollar days are as cherished as cougar encounters.

Planters have gathered for the off-season in certain parts of the country, in areas that have low insurable-weeks restrictions, where the skiing is good, or the nightlife is hot, or the dope grows green and abundant. The Kootenays are good. Or Montreal. Commercial Drive, Vancouver. Halifax. Sending out bi-weekly cards and receiving big fat cheques. All winter long. Others go abroad, hang on a beach in Guatemala while a buddy fills out the cards. If caught they only deduct the penalty from next year's claim. Ninety days work then $1,500 a month until the season starts again next spring.

Contracting outfits sometimes arrange their entire corporate structure around scoring pogey. The contractor can be an employee of a holding company, thereby getting weeks to qualify as well. A large crew is deftly juggled to lay off some when they get their weeks, hiring new planters the whole time to take up the slack. In the winter the holding company drops off to sleep and everyone is glued to their mailboxes.

Of course, planters did not dream up this kind of winter work. Mills have regular layoffs fully supported by UI. Loggers don't all work in the winter. Nationally, silviculture has been heavily subsidized by the federal government for years. Forests are a provincial concern, but the federal government, with a view to tidying up after the provinces, has funneled hundreds and hundreds of millions of dollars back into the system to replant all the unplanted shitholes. How many planters on UI do you need to get a hundred million dollars?

A million-tree contract can be knocked off by a good crew in less than a month. If the contractor holds onto a nickel per tree that's $50,000. No wonder you get all these half-baked outfits from the big city underbidding, doing a lousy job, maybe not paying their planters. This is what you read about treeplanting in *The Globe and Mail*, if you read about it at all.

four and one

Only rarely do real weekends exist in the treeplanting universe. Contract work becomes more profitable as the overall efficiency of operations increases. Planters rarely come from near where they are planting so there is really nothing very close to come home to.

Each day is part of a master agenda. A countdown to Christmas. A season is divided into the number of weeks required or shifts to be worked in order to become eligible for unemployment benefits. Shifts are broken down into the number of days. Four days on the job and one day off works well, each day off a different day of the week, perhaps a different town. Irregular schedules for an odd occupation. Six and one is not uncommon, with Tuesday night spent every time in Sioux Lookout or Zeballos. There is no greater struggle than waiting for the day off to arrive. And then it's gone. Sleep in, eat, do the laundry, sleep some more.

Irregular scheduling is indicative of the broader disregard for the traditional economy and work ethic. It's all part of the outcast mentality, living in exile. Self-imposed seclusion from all that is normal, regular, predictable. Planters pose a threat to normalcy. They don't belong to unions. They have their own language and separate habits. They represent too weird an alternative.

Although ultimately satisfying, this approach leads to some conflict whenever the two worlds meet in a bank back home, or in the parking lot outside the only bar in town when the crew shows up for a night off.

Getting beaten up is not a unique planter experience. It happens to fruitpickers. Gay bashing happens everywhere. But given the right conditions, the perfect bar, the ideal music, just that crucial blend of xenophobia, frustration, and drunkenness, there is nothing as frightening or as absurd as a couple of local guys kicking a treeplanter.

Imagine three or four angry drunks standing in a circle taking turns booting the teeth out of a planter who is possibly wired on mushrooms, having laughed too loud, or danced too much, or been too free. The expression "kicked him till your leg was sore," comes to mind. To a heavy-metal soundtrack, ribs broken, untallied score settled, one more time before the cops arrive.

the unofficial international perspective

Studying forestry, on a field trip, southern France. We stop the bus in the middle of a pine plantation that Napoleon supposedly started. Everyone crowds out to relieve themselves and observe the local silviculture techniques. A common farm tractor winds its way through the stumps, hydraulic dibble at the back making well-spaced mechanical holes, a man in a chair on the back suspended over all this action inserting seedlings and quickly covering over the holes as the tractor coughs. The ground is sandy and flat. The stumps are small, spaced at about two meters. Our group is visibly impressed by this display, though none of them know enough French to express their satisfaction to our host.

So I ask the guy, "On peux planter combien d'arbres comme ça?" and he says, "Ça dépend, peut être mille, douze cents dans une bonne journée." Twelve hundred trees?! I watch the tractor struggle to turn tightly around a stump, two guys to operate the belching rig, balloon tires like a dune buggy. In my best French I try to explain that with my underwear on the outside, a pair of Birkenstocks, and half a loaf of peanut butter and avocado sandwiches, I could jam around three thousand of the ungrateful little bastards into the ground, continually, day after day, eight runs of 400 like performing tai chi. Maybe it's my French. Or maybe it's my tone of voice, but our host looks at me like I'm making fun of him, and continues, through an interpreter, to explain the characteristics of this technique.

Yeah, but hold on here. I turn to the guy beside me, a retired forester from New South Wales. I relate the discussion that I've just had, asking him if this makes any sense. His smile widens, and I can see the miles of radiata pine that he has administered reflecting in his eyes. "Twelve hundred trees? That's pretty good I reckon. We'd budget on about 800 ... mind you it's hillier in Oz."

Two guys and a souped-up Massey-Ferguson putting in a thousand trees. An absolute creamshow. I turn back to watch the tractor and assume the position in my mind: the blade of my shovel slicing open the appropriate hole, the tree in the left hand slipping into place, straight and buried up to its neck, toeing it in as I move onto the next one. The effortless dance, occupational aerobics, juggling the specific movements and the exacting specifications with the economy of exertion that evolves from performing the same task a million times.

The tractor turns at the end of a row and with a sputter and wheeze stops for lunch. As we load into our bus I become entangled in the mathematics of comparative production rates, wondering why the hell treeplanting as we know it is such a big secret.

John Cathro is a former treeplanter who lives in the Kootenays, BC. He now works for a forestry company trying to reduce the amount of clearcut logging.

The Treeplanter's Experience

Photographs by Hélène Cyr

Photographer's Note

The quotes from treeplanters and other captions for the photographs are not the words, or necessarily the sentiments, of those people who are shown in the images. The photographs were taken over a period of five years from 1989 through to 1994, plus a day in 1998. All images are full frame, taken with Kodak film, and printed on Ilford paper.

The inspiration for these pictures has been my strong desire to record the devastation of the forests and to portray the lives of the treeplanters who try to bandage these wounds. This lifestyle, as we know it, may soon be a thing of the past.

Goals surround planting. The tree line in the distance becomes emblematic of so many achievements we dream of as we bend down over and over and over. In all its uncertainty, pain, and beauty, in its blissful hell, planting is eternally etched on my personal history.
ANDREW PARKER

Why is treeplanting so strenuous? Based on planting 1,600 trees per day, a treeplanter:
- Lifts a cumulative weight of over 1,000 kilograms
- Bends more that 200 times per hour
- Drives the shovel into the ground more than 200 times per hour
- Travels about 16 kilometers on foot while carrying heavy loads of seedlings.
WORKERS' COMPENSATION BOARD

As Sal gently explained to me, I had to let go of my ladylike restraint and attack the ground like the mosquitoes were attacking me. Stride stride probe probe screef screef—JAB!—open insert—STOMP! Stride to the next spot. It took him as long to do it as it does to say it. I wept and tried to hide it as I watched him plant in minutes what I'd been carrying around for hours. Soon, when I was considered "trained," my whiny outpourings were met with a friendly "shut up and plant" from the lifers — words I now apply to all my life's troubles that can be solved with simple determination and hard work. Just shut up and plant.
JALEEN GROVE

At home in Nova Scotia when the tide is low in the Bay of Fundy, you can walk down the mud flats to a petrified forest which is around three million years old. All that's left are gray stone stumps sticking a foot out of the water. In British Columbia the petrified forests on the clearcuts are created in a matter of months by cutting in the winter. They stand on charred rocks from which the soil has been washed away to nourish those stone trees in the sea.
MEG SIRCOM

A lot of today's jobs are about taking and exploiting in one way or another. Treeplanting is about giving, combined with hardship. When you leave the field, you're also leaving a part of yourself behind.
SERGE GAMACHE

Physical ability peaks in five weeks, then fatigue or burnout occurs. Most common ailments are back pain, sunburn, skin irritation, diarrhea, insomnia, chronic fatigue, and depression.

In 1997 in British Columbia, over 300 silviculture contracting companies had almost 15,000 employees on their payrolls.

Welcome to gumbo city. All through northern Alberta and Saskatchewan, and parts of BC,
there is a particular kind of mud — gumbo — that sticks to your shovel like a dead weight
one day and the next day is as hard as cement.

Unlikely as it sounds, some planters have a little energy to burn off after dinner.

Some days I had to frequently reconsider what my motivations were for being there, for planting the next tree. Money, although the reason for my trying out treeplanting, was not the element that would help me keep going once on the block.
MARIE-PIERRE GERMAIN

46

Some slower planters do services for the faster planters, not for cash, but in exchange for a portion of their daily tree count. By taking on chores such as washing socks or doing dish duties, a slower planter can increase his or her tree score. The laundry service is a little slow, but the view is magnificent.

It is not uncommon to have absolutely no idea where on earth you are.

A certain brand of teamwork is crucial when passing the bulk of the work from hand to hand.

The cookshack smells like home, with a stereo in the corner and mud underfoot.
If you can't find what you need in here, then you don't need it or it doesn't exist.

Meetings are like the six o'clock news. Planters need to know how many more trees must be planted to complete the contract, the percentage of planted trees which passed the quality check, and, more importantly, when the next shipment of cigarettes, booze, and gummy bears will arrive.

Treeplanters "veg" the best. They are really good at lying back and doing nothing because
their bodies are just too tired to do anything else.
JIM PHILLIPOFF

There's no better place to search for that perfect chord than standing on the edge of the block.

Carpooling home at the end of another day at the office.

A functional, funky village for 30 people can be broken into pieces
and loaded on to the back of the truck in a matter of hours.
Planters can be kind of like ants.

Treeplanting is about endurance, not physical but mental. It can mean solitude, thirst, blackened nails, and frustration. Or perhaps poor management, bad food, and complicated politics. But ultimately whether you fail or succeed is up to you.
KAREN HENRION

Average daily production:
• 1,301 trees per day; 7.2 hours per day
• 182 trees per hour; 3 trees per minute; 1 tree every 20 seconds (not including walking)
• 442 trees per load; 31.9 lbs. per load
• heart rate of 132 beats per minute.

Bad block.
Soaked to the bone and 16 cents a tree in knee-high grass
with a compulsory one-square-foot bootscreef.
The top highballer only managed 600 trees. Ninety-six dollars.

I will never forget the time I took off my boot and threw it into an afternoon so thick with bugs that I could see the tunnel of its trajectory. My feet hurt. My wrists hurt. My skin hurt. Still, I know my grandchildren will see the trees and be glad I did it. I will tell them about the bugs and the bosses and it will sound like stories of the war my grandfather told me. It was war, another children's crusade. We did it because we had to, and even though it was hell, it had a kind of peace that was hard to leave behind. Every time.
SASHA ROGERS

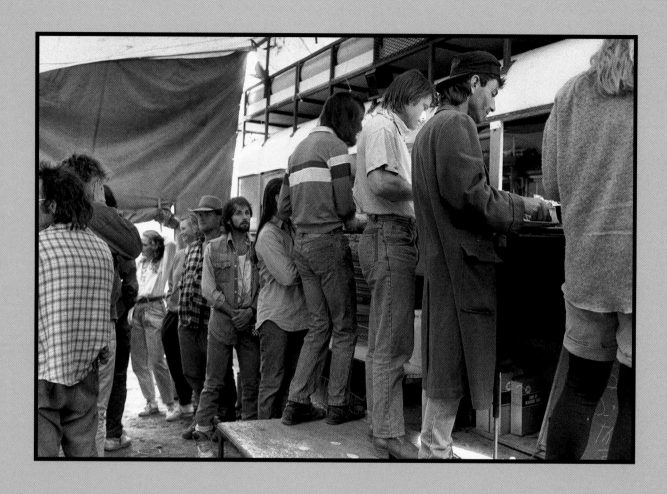

For a camp fee of $20-a-day or more you can eat as much great food as possible
and still have room for a second piece of pie.

The first and most enduring lesson I learned about cooking for a treeplanting camp was an equation for determining the quantity of food for 50 planters: if a recipe claims to feed six hungry people, count each treeplanter as three regular people, multiply the recipe 18 times (or until you're certain that the amount will be way more than necessary), then make two times that amount. Cooking and baking for 50 people who eat like 150 people taught me to scoff at delicate measuring directions. Within my first week I'd discarded the teaspoon measure. Never once did I even flip open the perforated "shaker" side of the spice container.
JENN ENRICO

On days off some people head for town, pizza, new socks, a pay phone, insoles, candles, matches, tobacco ... the list is endless. Others stay in camp and try to catch up on sleep, conversation, and personal grooming.

Another activity on days off is mending bags and boots or modifying equipment.
Some planters file their shovels every other day to keep the blades smooth
and thereby reduce the strain on their arms.

Here we come from different walks of life; we have different ideas, opinions, and pretenses and yet we accept one another. Here the work we do is intense and so are our social interactions. Words are not wasted in idle chitchat but are savored, used selectively, and in greater depth. Here we see all the things we are normally too busy to notice: a good meal, a drink of water, a warm bed, a cool breeze, a human touch. Here we try and spark the growth of the forest, and somewhere in the midst of it all we have sparked growth in ourselves.
TAMMY BAERG

To the planters:
I know that you've never worked, played, drunk, or eaten so well or so hard,
for so long, in such little time as you did in camp. I also know, from 15 years of camp cooking, that you
have suffered the consequences and learned two of the most valuable lessons for a harmonious
life and death — clean up your mess and don't pig out on the cookies!
CONNIE L. ROCK

Depending on the ground, a crew of 25 planters can pound in 30 or 40,000 trees a day.
Trees are packed 250 to a box. Transporting all these boxes can take forever and is not generally paid work.

A foreman's job is thankless and often only witnessed by the blackflies.

Treeplanting fashion is definitely dictated by bugs. When I planted in Ontario,
some of the highballers dressed for "the office." They wore "white" long-sleeved dress shirts and neckties.
The ties kept the bugs from crawling down their necks, and they sealed all buttoned openings
with velcro or duct tape. It was quite a look.
BRENDA WARDLE

Women comprise 50 percent of the population of British Columbia but only:
• 45 percent of the provincial labor force
• 12 percent of the forest industry workforce
• 12 percent of British Columbians who earn more than $50,000 per year
• 25 percent of silviculture workers.

The physical exertion level and work efficiency of treeplanters is among the highest
ever recorded in human occupational performance studies. In fact, they measured treeplanters
with relative exertion levels that were 75 percent of an Olympic marathoner.
WESTERN SILVICULTURE CONTRACTORS ASSOCIATION

Since the first seedling was planted in 1930:
• Over four billion seedlings have been planted in British Columbia
• Over ten billion seedlings have been planted in Canada
Since 1981 three billion seedlings have been planted in British Columbia.

When it hit me, it hit me hard ... driving, pissing rain, so cold that I could barely grip my shovel,
let alone plant. Frozen, miserable, and full of self-pity, I stood sandwiched between two highballers
moving with robotic precision. Then I humbly knew I would and could never be one of them.
Beaten, I surrendered and flagged down the van. There was always tomorrow.
SANDRA LEE

"Should I stay or should I go?"... hurry up and wait ... a fascinating mixture of people, character, and culture.
Probably the toughest mental and physical job one will ever do.
Altogether a unique lifetime experience.
MARTIN BEGIN

Waiting for dinner at the end of a long hard day.

The dreams of treeplanters drift in from the depths of complete exhaustion,
always accompanied by obscure scenes of the job, and almost never lasting long enough.

Days of monotonous hard work stretch out endlessly. I think this is why the simple pleasures bring me so much joy when they dot the days of drudgery. The grandeur of the northern landscape, the refreshing wave of a cool breeze on a hot day, the warmth of being recipient of a spontaneous smile, the sweetness of an orange, the delicious feeling of being clean after a hot shower, the comfort of lying down to sleep — things like these bring a genuine happiness and are often taken for granted when I am in the city. Just as the hardships become exaggerated, so do the good times and simple pleasures.
ALTHEA THAUBERGER

I have always enjoyed the intense solitude of treeplanting. No matter how much of a tribe
every camp is, ultimately it's all up to you. You can sit on a log all day and curse the weather, the bugs,
your soaking, aching feet, or you can just keep moving and get those trees in the ground.
After a good day you really feel alive.
ALISON BROOMAN

Cooks wake at 4:30 a.m. or earlier to prepare both breakfast and the lunch table.
Once the planters have left for the block, cooks may nap until early afternoon. By 2 or 3 p.m.
they begin to prepare dinner, a meal which consists of soup, salad, main courses which
are meat-based, vegetarian, or even vegan, and finally dessert.
Cooks burn out fast.

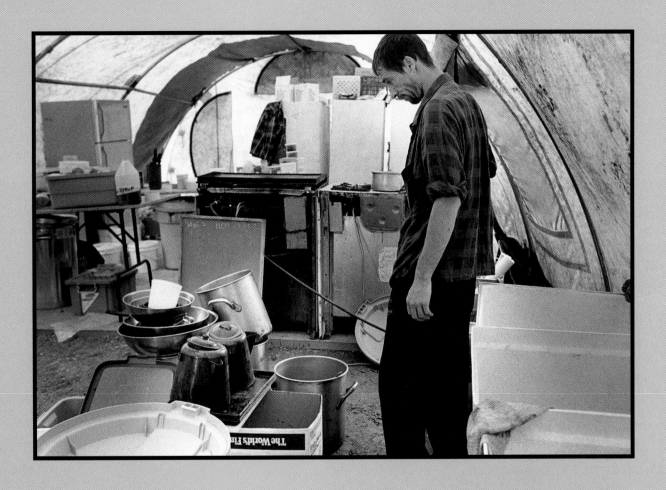

Dish duty: 40 forks, knives and spoons; 40 bowls; 40 plates; 40 cups; and never-ending pots and pans. Two hours of your evening.

It's amazing how many people in a planting camp can play and sing very well.

Music fits in to every moment of the day.
There is usually someone willing to play or sing and always someone who wants to listen.

Nothing in city life can be compared to the intense euphoria felt on the last day of planting, leaving camp for the last time, and thinking this will be the last season.

A contractor's association survey revealed that 37 percent of the work force are students while 30 percent of workers are more than 30 years old.

Many treeplanting contractors avoid the hassles of building and maintaining wilderness camps, and instead arrange lodging for their planters in motels with kitchen units. They then drive their planters anywhere up to an hour and a half each way to and from the block.

Motel "shows" can be both comfortable and challenging.
Hot showers and a bug-free environment more than compensate for the morning ride to the block.
But it is difficult to find the time and energy to buy your food, cook it, eat it, and have a shower,
after working a ten-hour day.

This year I had a relapse and went treeplanting again. Not that I ever considered myself a treeplanter; it was just something I had to do for money. On chance meetings with "authentic" treeplanters at a bar somewhere nicely removed from planting, outlandish stories are exchanged. They are all true, always entertaining, and described with an exuberance that I have never encountered outside the treeplanting experience. I will never miss the planting, but I'll always feel cheated if whatever I do next hasn't the same exuberance. This is all I care to come away with after ten years of denying the fact that I am a treeplanter.

JEAN-FRANÇOIS CYR

Foremen work extremely long hours. They are always on call for emergencies and they deny themselves sleep by assuming responsibilities that start long before the planters set off for the block and finish long after the planters are asleep.

Each year on public and private land in Canada, government and industry spend
$800 million on silviculture.

As I sit here now (months after treeplanting), I find myself still processing the events of the previous summer. The time I spent treeplanting in northern BC helped me to better evaluate my life, to figure out what I want and what direction I may take. Many of the friends I made while planting have become my family. I live with four other planters. It's strange to me that the many hardships I encountered have faded from my memory and when I reflect on my planting experience I do so with a smile. Treeplanting has left me a stronger woman, both physically and mentally, and I feel a sense of empowerment that has followed me out of the bush.

KATHERINE BARKLEY

Many blocks are not accessible to vehicles.
Needless to say, the planters are rarely paid for the walk in.

Bagging up — a time when sighs and encouraging words are heard, when you smoke anything
with intensity, cram two sandwiches down and possibly five more cookies, industrial quantities of water,
gummy bears, and bee pollen or whatever is in fashion that year.

One time when I was planting in the Queen Charlottes, it was so steep that I was slightly off balance. The ground was pretty slashy with lots of green. I leaned back a bit too far and suddenly I did a complete back flip. I looked around me; all my trees were in the bag and I was on my feet exactly 2.9 meters — the contract spacing — away from the last tree. So I planted my next tree and just kept on going.
JIM PHILLIPOFF

It's a continual challenge, even for the most experienced planter, to correctly space off the last planted tree when it is camouflaged by debris and shoulder-high slash.

"How did you end up here? I thought you were below the road."

Treeplanters always talk about working in the bush.
But technically, if you're working in the bush, you've gone too far.
MIKE MacINTYRE

Treeplanters thrive on adversity.
SCOTT CHISHOLM

The reforestation industry group that includes treeplanters has an average
annual rate of about 22 injury claims per 100 workers. Injuries to the wrists and back
combined make up almost half of all reported injuries.
WORKERS' COMPENSATION BOARD

Tailgate party, wondering who is going to be the first to get up and go back to work.

For four months of the year I wake at 5:30, eat, travel, plant, drive, eat, and sleep.
My fellow planters become entangled with my own battered, rank body in the crewcab, just as my hands
become adopted by soil. The repetitive days help to clear my mind of all the
information gathered throughout the winter.
KIRSTEN HOLKESTAD

Footgear is one of the major issues for treeplanters. Leather caulks, rubber caulks, half-and-half caulks, running shoes, or Birkenstocks — it doesn't matter what you wear, your feet will always hurt and you should have worn the boots you left in camp.

The art of removing the thorns of devil's club, brambles, and wild roses takes patience and practice.

So much of a treeplanter's day is spent trying to do more than two things at the same time.

In our camp near Gold River in 1974, we had 28 planters (14 men, 14 women) two cooks,
and five children in diapers. Every day one person stayed in camp to be the babysitter and every
other day someone stayed home to bake 28 loaves of whole-wheat bread in a woodstove.
DAVID BOEHM

Sometimes even duct tape is not enough to hold it all together.

If you don't look after your hands, the tiny cuts which you get on your fingers from repeatedly thrusting them into the ground, soon become red, swollen, cracked, and painful and could cost you $50 a day in lost production. Look after your hands.

Round and bubbly, weariness weighs on my soul. I'm glad for the time to rest and repair.
Deep below is the contentment of a hard day's labor, finding pleasure in everyday occurrences,
a life beautiful in its lack of excess.
MICHAEL FISHER

Treeplanting is a social but, at the same time, solitary activity completely removed from the mainstream culture. It allows people from all over the country and of diverse backgrounds and experience to come together and participate in something unique: hard labor under adverse, stressful conditions in a devastated natural environment. The rewards are immense and more than simply monetary. Many aspects of the job require an inner revolution on the part of the planter. The possibility of personal development and the chance of a new and richer sense of fulfilment make the hard road traveled by planters a little more comforting.
PAUL RAVEN

Each year 200 million seedlings are planted in British Columbia, 120 million in Ontario, and 190 million in Quebec. In Canada as a whole, 650 million seedlings are planted each year.

The area clearcut in Canada in the last 20 years is roughly equal to the size of Washington State.
The area clearcut in BC in the past 20 years is roughly equal to the size of Vancouver Island,
only slightly smaller than Switzerland.

For me the most challenging part of planting used to be its physical demands.
That's become the manageable part. Now it's trying to stay sane while doing the same repetitive
motions and doing them in the rain, the heat, and the bugs, day after day. Doing this job has always
presented me with something to master in myself. It has taught me how to work hard, both
physically and mentally, and that carries over into everything I do.
CHARLOTTE GILL

After working eight hours in the hot sun no amount of liquid will quench the thirst.

At the end of the day, the foreman takes the scores — the number of trees planted by each person.
Reporting your score is based on the honor system and it is a matter of pride and
personal integrity that you are honest about the number planted.
Everyone will lose if the books don't balance at the end of the contract.

8:40 a.m.: Already planted 240 trees at 21 cents each. On track for another $300 day.

In no other job will you leave town at 5 a.m., drive for one hour, ride a boat for two hours, and fly in a helicopter before setting up camp. Treeplanting is like a marathon.
STEPHANE LEDUC

"I forgot. Are we going to work or are we coming home?"

These are memories you will have for life. Treeplanting is a life of extremes.
You cannot work harder, be more tired, or have more fun.

I recommend treeplanting occasionally to people I dislike or those with masochistic tendencies.
Good money if you can't think of a better way to make it. Repetitive, hard, physical labor in an often
disorganized work environment isn't my idea of fun. I don't miss it much except for an amazing
cook named Mona, a few good parties, and some pretty French girls.
ROB URSEL

Pretensions don't last.
Relationships develop at light speed. In such raw conditions,
never have I seen people more eloquent.
DAVID STEWART

Many relationships start on the treeplanting blocks.
What's more, there are thousands and thousands of children out there who have been
conceived in the duff. I have two.
DAVID BOEHM

People come from all corners of the globe — two Russian friends pose proudly.

There are 15 different fungicides, insecticides, and herbicides commonly applied to
bare-root and container-stock plugs in British Columbia seedling nurseries.
It is not uncommon to have six different pesticides applied to seedlings before they are planted.
As of 1994, 25,000 hectares of land were sprayed each year with chemicals to control
brush competition on British Columbia plantations.

Hurry up and wait for the trees to be delivered, or the helicopter to arrive,
or the urge to go back and plant.

Treeplanting is for the insane.
CORRIE DESILETS

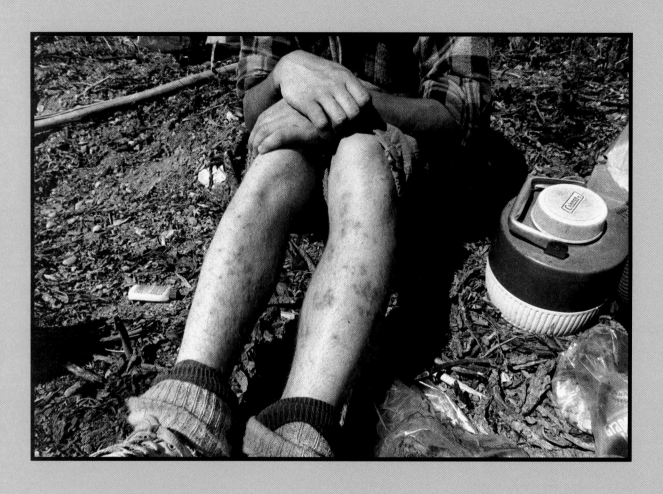

It's humbling to realize that you are nothing more than mosquito food.
MICHAEL PASIKOV

It has been said that you are only as happy as your feet. For the treeplanter it's the hands. Hangnails, blisters, and the claw get worse with each tree planted.

Mud, rain, hail, mud, sleet, snow, mud, ice, wind, mud, rain, mud — and the most
beautiful rainbow, people, life! Not to be missed!
LEONARD WEAVER

The British Columbia Ministry of Forests has built over 40,000 kilometers of road.
The British Columbia Ministry of Transportation and Highways has built and maintains
27,000 kilometers of paved road.

Every planter has wondered this: why does the simplest thing have to be so damned epic?

The rear rotor of the helicopter turns at twice the speed of sound.
The pilot says, "Stay away from the back of the machine or you'll mess up the blade."

The more one looks at the big picture of forest mismanagement the more angry one becomes.
It's hard not to be cynical about planting. Planting is the end of the whip of the harvest model.
We planters struggle amidst all that is destructive and ugly about logging, struggle to apply an obviously
inadequate poultice on our earth, struggle to finish a season without injury, struggle to
collect our pay — and we struggle with our consciences. What treeplanter wouldn't happily
give it up tomorrow to end clearcutting today?
ROB SIMPSON

The first time I went planting, my birthday was on a wet, slushy day during which it took us 3 ½ hours to drive 14 kilometers to a new block, and 1 ½ hours to return through the same, by now drier, mud. My second year planting, I spent my birthday in a very smelly swamp. The third year planting, my birthday fell on one of a series of icy days. I was put into someone else's ground to finish after they had creamed it out. It was probably one of my worst days ever. My fourth planting birthday, I spent five hours driving around logging roads trying to find a new camp. The day ended with bread and peanut butter and sleeping in the van at the side of the highway
ZUZANA VASKO

Drinking beer, smoking joints, and sitting around an open fire.
You know you should be sleeping, but you just can't — you're having too much fun.

Treeplanting is something I would rather look back on than ever do again.
I have seen paradise ruined by clearcuts. I have gone to bed aching and dirty and covered with bites.
I have been so badly blistered by the sun that my face stuck to my pillow while I slept.
I have been ripped off by bosses. Those pictures are history. I am an elder in the tribe, part of a mural,
twelve guys in a rented room on our day off, sharing a bottle and food.
KEEFER ROGERS

End-of-contract photo opportunities are harder to organize than everything else combined.

Just when you think the job couldn't get any stranger, three people crawl out of the swamp and become Greek statues.

Ten billion trees have been planted in Canada in the last 25 years.
At an average of 1,500 trees per hectare, this would cover almost 66,000 square kilometers —
an area larger than almost half of the world's countries, including Costa Rica, Denmark, and Israel.

In 1981, the survival rate among planted seedlings in British Columbia was 58 percent. Today the survival rate is 85 percent.

If you can plant trees, you can do anything.
NIKLAUS ANTHONISEN

Glossary

back cut: A forceful jab and twist just behind the tree with the shovel to close the bottom of the hole.

bags: Tree-carrying gear with straps like a backpack, worn on the hips, made out of plastic-coated canvas.

bag out: Emptying the bags of trees. A constant goal to be reached as quickly as possible.

bag up: Filling the bags with a couple of hundred seedlings at the cache on the side of the road. Bagging up is the best opportunity to eat, drink, smoke, talk, laugh, and lie around, and can be performed in less than a minute when the going is good.

bare root: Originally, seedlings were grown in real soil, uprooted after a year, tied into bundles with their roots hanging down.

beach: How it feels when the soil is soft and free of roots and rock. True beaches are very rare, usually small, and always planted immediately.

block: See cutblock.

bootscreef: The removal of organic material from a microsite by use of one large boot to reveal mineral soil or other suitable planting medium. Bootscreefing can be a lot faster than shovel screefing, but is slower than not screefing at all.

bootin' up: An activity that occurs somewhere between breakfast and the first run of the day and is usually accompanied by a sincere groaning noise.

bong: A waterpipe for smoking pot or hash or both.

bug dope: Insect repellent, also called deet, perfume, cologne, and insect attractant. Bug dope always ends up in the planters' eyes, so is rarely used except in exceptional circumstances.

cache: Where the trees are kept, under a tarp, on the side of the road. The cache contains lunches, water bottles, rain gear, old gloves, and boxes or baskets or bags of trees.

caulks: Pronounced "corks," these are the little spikes that screw into the soles of boots like cleats on golf shoes, and help prevent the planter from slipping.

checker (the): The silviculture technician who conducts quality surveys on behalf of the logging company or the government. Planting experience is not a prerequisite to being a checker, so the opportunities for difference of opinion are many.

claw: It is not uncommon to have to pry open the fingers very slowly in the morning in order to use the hand. A tight grip on the shovel, and constant bashing against rocks, can bring on the claw in a couple of days.

cream: Creamshow. La crème. Gravy. Those parts of the block where the planting is very fast, relative to the bid price. The word "cream" is generally applied to expanses of open dirt, roadsides, fire guards, and other spots where velocity of production is well above average.

crummy: The chariot. An old logging expression for the banged-up excuse for a rig in which people ride to work. There is no harder job for a truck than carrying a load of treeplanters up dirt roads.

cull: A seedling that arrives from the nursery so damaged that it has to be thrown away rather than planted. Obviously there is a sliding scale between plantable and dead; the field definition depends sometimes on the mood and the weather as much as the state of the tree.

cutblock: The place of employment in the opening in the forest. Also known as the clearcut, the slope, the block, and the end of the earth.

dibble: Once the planting tool of choice, a dibble is a long stick with a round metal end just slightly larger in diameter than the plug.

dirt shot: Wide open, unobstructed blast for the cash. This is the cutblock equivalent of a "gimme." It's always tempting to try and squeeze two trees into one dirt shot.

duct tape: The usual wide, silver wonder affixer. Everyone carries a roll or knows where to get one pretty quick. It can be used to hold rain gear in one piece, fix the cassette player, cover a wound, or help plumb the sauna.

duff: This decomposing organic material is what a screef is intended to remove in order to expose a plantable spot. Duff ranges in depth from the slightest skiff on top of deep soil to a bottomless layer of rotting wood.

fill plant: Planting in a partially stocked block. Fill plants occur either where the natural regeneration is considered insufficient, or where the previously planted trees are dead.

foreman: Also known as foreperson, forehead, foreskin, four-by. The foreman is basically a truck driver, line cutter, nose wiper, tree counter, and personal secretary to the five or ten planters on a crew. Some foremen have the same crew year after year, and have songs written about them.

four and one: A common planting schedule, measured in days on and off, stretching from one end of the season to the next, with a few days thrown in here and there to change contracts or move camp.

greasy black: The state that organic soil must be in to be considered plantable. A point of constant discussion between planters and checkers, greasy black is typically fast to plant and occurs less frequently than most planters claim.

gumbo: What most of Canada would look like if you drove trucks back and forth over it during the wettest time of year. A completely bizarre combination of silt, clay, and organics that is stickier than snot. Sometimes referred to as crew glue.

highballer: The fastest planter — so fast that nobody else even comes close. In its most general sense, there are a couple of highballers on every crew. In its purest sense, there are only about a half dozen true highballers in the history of treeplanting.

j-root: Acceptable roots and plugs must be planted vertically in the hole. J-roots are a common fault, and at times may appear to be capable of spontaneously occurring after the planter has moved on to the next tree.

landing: A wide spot in the road where logs were loaded on to trucks and where planters usually set up a cache. Landings at the very end of logging roads are like clearcut cul-de-sacs and are home to the full range of planter activity.

microsite: The specific patch of earth into which a tree is planted. Microsites are often created by screefing. The proper condition of a microsite is a point of much discussion among planters and checkers.

mineral soil: What is usually considered to be the only appropriate planting medium into which a tree may be planted. There never seems to be enough mineral soil on the block.

naturals: Trees on the edge and in the middle of cutblocks that have not been planted by treeplanters. Planted trees may be planted at contract spacing, or adjacent to, naturals, depending on whether the natural is regarded as a crop tree.

organics: Somewhere directly between duff and greasy black. Organics are not always an allowable microsite, but it sure would be nice if they were.

plugs: Most trees planted these days are grown in huge nurseries with their roots in slender containers so as to form a root plug.

quad: Four-wheeled all-terrain vehicle, used mostly by the tree runner to deliver boxes of seedlings to the crew across rough ground. Quads also make OK toys if there is nothing better to do.

red rot: Course, chunky decomposing wood from logging slash. Red rot is somewhere between a fallen tree and real dirt in the soil-building process. Certain types of red rot are considered to be plantable, so the line is often open to interpretation.

reefer: A refrigerated trailer where seedlings are stored. A reefer is also another name for a joint.

replant: One of the most dreaded words in the entire vocabulary. Ground has to be replanted if the first attempt was less than perfect.

rock pile: On a bad day, even a fairly good patch of ground can look like a rock pile, and every stab for dirt rings out with the wrist-buckling clang of the shovel hitting a buried boulder.

run: Everything that happens between bagging up and bagging out. In bad ground, the first run can take till lunch. On good ground it is possible to make eight or ten runs before lunch.

screef: Removing the organic layer from the soil using a shovel or a boot. It can take as little as half a second or as long as forever to screef the appropriate microsite according to the local specifications.

scarify: Screefing performed by bulldozers, skidders, and excavators in order to prepare the block for planting. Blocks can be scarified with furrows, trenches, mounds, or brackies, which are big scallops spaced in rows on flat ground.

shit pile: A widely applicable description of most of the places planters show up for work, though only truly appropriate for those blocks where the slash and rock make movement not only tortuously slow but also very dangerous.

shnarb: The mangled pieces of trees left on the block after the stems have been dragged to the road and loaded on to trucks. Shnarb appears to be designed to scratch, poke, grab, and tear at planters.

slash: Slash is all of the logs and branches and stumps and assorted shnarb that clutters up the block. Slash piles are sometimes twenty feet high, or bulldozed into wind rows hundreds of meters long, or simply left in an even blanket covering the ground.

stash: To stash trees is to hide them under the slash or bury them in the ground or throw them into the river by the bundle or the box. Stashing happens very rarely, and is widely seen as the lowest expression of planter decency.

tree line: The edge of the block, where clearcut blends back into forest, usually accompanied by a skid trail or a fire guard to further delineate it from the work place. The tree line is one of the many goals on which the planter sets his or her sights throughout the day.

tree runner: The person on the crew who is in charge of delivering trees from the reefer or the main cache to the individual planters on the block. Tree runners spend a lot of time in trucks, on quads, or driving back and forth from camp to the curling rink in town where the trees are sometimes kept.

Index of Images

New Society Publishers
specializes in books that contribute in fundamental ways
to ecological and social sustainability.
If you have enjoyed *Handmade Forests*,
you might also like the following titles:

ECOFORESTRY
**The Art and
Science of
Sustainable
Forest Use**
Edited by Alan
Drengson and
Duncan Taylor

FORESTS OF
HOPE
**Stories of
Regeneration**

by Christian Küchli

Ecoforestry focuses on the new paradigm in
forestry — the philosophy, goals, policy and
practices of ecologically and economically sustainable forest use, with contributions from James
Agee, Herb Hammond, Chris Maser, Nancy Turner,
Arne Naess, Gary Snyder, and others.

Filled with beautiful color photographs, *Forests of
Hope* takes the reader to 12 different countries
including Brazil, India, Tanzania, Costa Rica,
Switzerland, and the United States as author-
photographer-forester Christian Küchli seeks out
tales of hope for the world's forests.

8" x 9" 320 pages 50 photos and graphics
Pb US$24.95 / Can$29.95
ISBN 0-86571-365-0

8.5" x 11" 256 pages 175 color photos
Pb US$29.95 / Can$39.95
ISBN 0-86571-378-2

NEW SOCIETY PUBLISHERS
www.newsociety.com